CONVERSATION: 7 communication techniques and tactics to win small talks.

Mike Bray

Mike Bray

ISBN-13: 978-1542385954
ISBN-10: 1542385954

"Hello! First of all I want to thank you for buying this book, it really supports me in writing more of them because I can see you get the value you want. I really appreciate that, but as well, if you feel like this book gave you something new, or you see something that you do not like, I would be glad if you could give me your HONEST review on this book on amazon, so that I will know what you think of my books and improve them to the future. If you have any other questions do not hesitate to contact me on my e-mail mikebrayofficial@gmail.com and I will answer within few hours. Thank you very much!

CONTENTS

Table of Contents

Conversation

Introduction

From the beginning of the world human being and animals are communicating each moment. A world cannot be imagined without communication. In societies we communicate with one another, in the forests the tigers, snakes, ants, birds communicate with one another, but the modes of communication are different in different places and in different situations. People sometimes use verbal languages and sometimes use non-verbal signs to communicate, sometimes they communicate orally and sometimes in a written way.

The word communication has come from a Latin word "communis" which means to share. Communication is a process by which animals and human beings exchange their feelings with each other. In other words, communication is the way in which people and other animals transmit information. For communication to take place two parties are needed. Nowadays communication is much more than just listening and speaking. It is a two way process speaker sends the message and listener gives a feedback. Your communication is successful when your listener lets you know that your information is understood by him/ her.

CHAPTER 1

Effective communication

Effective communication and better social skills are fundamental to your success in every aspect of life. Almost every job requires people with strong communication skills and social people; and, it is easier to make friends, develop stronger relationships, and improve your career when your social skills are well adept.

If you lack good social skills, it's crucial to first learn how to build effective communication, and then proceed to improving your social skills.

When it comes to improving your communication skills, there are 3 areas that you should concentrate on especially if you experience social phobia.

1.Non-verbal communication

2.Conversation skills

3.Assertiveness

Nonverbal Communication

In many occurrences, the biggest part of what we communicate with other people is nonverbal. What you tell other people with your eyes and your body language tends to be as powerful as what you tell them with words. When you experience social phobia, you might behave in a way designed to avoid communication with others. For instance, avoiding eye contact or speaking too softly expresses that you are not ready to communicate.

Moreover, avoiding eye contact, speaking quietly or keeping a distance while talking to others will most likely communicate, "Stay away from me," or "I don't want to talk to you."

Below are steps that can help you identify your problem areas and improve your nonverbal communication skills.

How to Hack NonVerbal Communication

To develop effective and highly social nonverbal cues: Step 1: Identify Your Trouble Spots To identify your trouble spots, ask yourself the following questions Do I have issues with maintaining eye contact while speaking to others?

Do I smile excessively or too little out of being nervous?

Do I speak too fast when I am nervous?

Is my speaking voice timid?

Do I slouch?

Do I keep my head down?

After identifying your pitfalls, pay attention to the

following nonverbal behaviors.

Posture: lean forward, head up, and stay alert when speaking to someone Gestures and movement: keep your arms uncrossed Physical distance: stay closer to the people you are talking to Eye contact: make appropriate eye contact with the person you are talking to Facial expression: smile warmly Volume of voice: use a volume that can be easily heard.

Step 2: Practice and Experiment your NonVerbal Skills To practice the above nonverbal cues and make them part of your everyday life: Practice one skill at a time before moving to the next one.

If you like, ask a friend or relative to comment on your nonverbal behavior. Then use the feedback to know how you appear to others while talking.

Videotape yourself communicating so you can be able to work on your trouble body cues appropriately.

Practice your new nonverbal skill in front of a mirror.

Once you practice using the correct nonverbal skill at home, experiment in real social situations, but consider starting out small with colleagues, tellers, or clerks.

Assertiveness

Assertiveness is the honest expression of someone's own feelings, wants, and needs, while still respecting others. If you experience social phobia, you definitely have a hard time expressing your feelings and thoughts openly. Assertive communication helps you to relate to other people more genuinely without resentment.

How to Develop Assertive Communication Skills

If you're socially awkward, you probably find it hard to request for something you want, and often feel as if you don't have the right to request whatever you desire. This is often because of an immense fear of feedback.

You can conquer such fear and become immensely assertive by: When you are making a request, start by showing you understand the other person's situation. For instance, "I know you probably had a lot to do lately…"

Next, define the situation in terms of how you feel about it. For instance, "this report is due next week on Tuesday, and I feel too overwhelmed at the moment, I am worried I won't be able to submit it by then."

Moreover, express your feelings rather than making accusations, i.e. "I often feel offended whenever you show up late to my office" rather than, "You always come to my office late! You don't even care about me!"

Be as brief and positive as you can while describing what you would like to happen. "I would like to discuss how we can share our work responsibilities."

Do you have trouble while expressing your views openly? Or often wait until others give their opinion first? Being assertive helps you own 'your own' opinion, i.e. "my personal view is it was unjust for her to mock you in front of your colleagues."

Armed with the knowledge of how to use various effective communication skills, let us now look at ways to improve your social skills.

Chapter 2.

5 Ways To Develop Effective Social

Skills

Developing good social skills helps in leading a happy, healthy, and enjoyable life. Research has proven that there is a positive association between your mental health and social skills. When you improve your social skills, you become more confident, charming, and nurture the ability to cultivate healthier relationships.

Anyone can effortlessly improve his/her social skills with practice and self-reflection. Here are the 5 steps to get you started in improving your social skills.

Practice

Just like any other skill, developing good social skills is a matter of practice. Introduce yourself to new people, converse with them, and get to know them. By doing this, you will develop your intuition about other people, and simultaneously become good at attuning to them to create a connection with them.

You may feel as if you should avoid social situations since you think you lack good social skills; this will only make you more anxious of social situations and you will have a hard time interacting with people. The key is to interact as much as you can.

Take Risks

Take risks by deliberately interacting with others. By this, I mean expressing your true feelings and thoughts as well as behaving in an authentic way. This is crucial because if you just stick to being restricted during social situations, you will not experiment and discover the possibilities; this makes it hard to improve your social skills.

Ask For Feedback

It's hard to work on your social skills when you don't have an idea of how others see you, and the effect certain nonverbal cues have on them. Ask other people to give you feedback according to their perspective on how you relate socially, on both your weaknesses and strengths. This will help you improve on any poor social skills into better and effective social skills.

Interact With People Who Are Socially Skilled

One good way to improve your social skills is by trying to model others. When you inter-relate with people who have good social skills, you can study their mannerism and learn from them.

Therefore, seek to hang out with individuals who are people savvy and with time; your social skills will begin to grow Work On Specific Goals

While there are a wide range of social skills, trying to improve all of them at once does not yield results. Pick one at a time and work on improving it. After you make good progress, proceed to another. This way, you will not only be building your social skills, but also building specific social skills that interest you.

Chapter 3.

Building Social Confidence-How To Do It

By now, you should have learnt quite a lot about overcoming social phobia and have started to embrace social situations little by little. In this chapter, we are going to look at how you can work on your confidence so that you can be able to start a conversation and keep it going.

To build social confidence: Create a Confident Outlook To create a confident look, you first must accept who you are, i.e. accept your personality and the person you are. Social phobias start at introversion; meaning you find comfort from being alone or spending time alone. If that description fits your personality, don't push yourself to be a more social or outgoing person because that's not who you are. In fact, if you try to be someone you are not, this may lead to anxiety, resentment, and stress. Instead, go to events, and social places that offer something you're interested in. For example, if you like reading, go to a written word event.

Accepting your true nature will help you focus on the value of your social connections.

Improve Social Competence You can easily become socially confident by engaging others in a mutually interesting manner where the other person has to get involved in the conversation. According to research, improving your social skill increases the level of positive self-awareness and acceptance in social situations. A positive perception of the 'self' enhances your confidence.

Avoid Negative Self Talk When you experience social phobia, you look for evidence that confirms your own beliefs because we like it when experiences match our predictions. Reprogram any situation that tries to challenge your self-perception. Whenever your thoughts navigate towards negative thinking, question these thoughts and look for evidence to approve or disapprove your negative thought; often, there will be an evidence deficit.

For instance, you are out for drinks and a thought pops up in your mind, "I know people here find me boring since I am not charming or charismatic". Stop such a thought and look for proof that approves or disapproves your thought.

Test Your Beliefs When you begin looking for evidences that support your feelings, analyze the evidence to find out whether the negative thoughts are in or out of your control. If not, let go; if so, do something about changing the situation. It's not good to assume that all external reactions are your fault.

Realize that others react out of their own fears, anxieties, and beliefs. For instance, perhaps you saw someone contorting his or her face and you immediately assume that the person is not interested in what you were telling them. Here is a thought; perhaps the person is feeling unwell or anxious about something else. Always ask yourself whether the attributes were for other things before taking them personal.

Let us now move on to learning the art of small talk so that you can strike a conversation with a stranger easily.

Chapter 4.

Mastering The Art Of Small Talk

Did you know there's nothing small about small talk. We often tend to think that making small talk is all about passing time or avoiding awkwardness. One thing we don't know is that many relationships and great friendships started with a discussion about the environment or weather.

Good small talk will not only enable you to build strong bonds but is also a crucial skill that can benefit you in your professional life. So how can you improve your ability of making small talk? If you are shy, socially anxious, introverted, or often feel uncomfortable amidst strangers, making small talk can become a stressful task. Sometimes, you may end up standing in silence while trying to avoid eye contact.

Fortunately, there is a technique you can use to guide you through this awkward moment and help you develop an ideal conversation that can establish relationships in the future.

The FORM Small Talk Trick

FORM represents Family, Occupation, Recreation, and Money. The idea behind the form trick is that the 4 topics can easily open up a conversation for you. These topics can help you delve into a conversation that has shared interest topics.

Family: talking about family tends to be a common experience; everyone has something to say about family without being too personal. For instance, "do you have kids?" "Where is your family from," etc.

Occupation: this is another open and relaxed topic to talk about. "Have you always been a soccer player?" "What do you do for a living?" "What is that like?"

Recreation: These are questions outside work. "What do you do when you are free?" What is your favorite TV show, movie, website?

Money: here, ask anything that is currently taking place

and falling into neutral field. "What do you think about the new liquor store's laws?" or "By the way, what happened with the price of car fuel?"

After adapting the FORM small trick, you can integrate other topics to what it stands for. For instance, M can be media instead of "money", and discuss anything that is happening in media. O can be "Olympics" and discuss everything about upcoming games, R can be "reading" and talk about what you have read recently, and F can be "fun," what they do for fun and so on.

In addition to the FORM technique, there is also the ARE technique. Let us look closely at this technique.

ARE Small Talk Technique

This simple technique stands for A: anchor, R: reveal, E: encourage. It has simple steps you can follow to start up a conversation with anyone.

Step 1: Anchor An anchor is an observation on mutual shared reality with others. It enables you to extend a conversation between you and the stranger. In this step, you only target to talk about something light or chat about something you are both experiencing or seeing.

"This weather is gorgeous"

"Dr. Cruse is hilarious"

"This music is just awesome"

Your anchor should not be a deep thought. Rather, it should be a polite and gradual talk to segue into a conversation.

Step 2: Reveal The next step is to bring up something about you that is related to the anchor you previously discussed. For instance, "I have tried to go along with DR. Cruse for the last two semesters now, and I've just come to understand him", "I have been waiting for such weather to go for an adventure." "The music today is much better than it was last night."

Opening up a little more allows you to extend the connection and the trust to the other person; this at the same time provides them something to which to respond.

17

Step 3: Encourage The last step is to keep the conversation rolling by asking them questions. Once you ask a question, proceed to mix it with comments; don't turn the conversation into an interview. Contribute more questions than comments, so that the other person may feel you are curious about them.

The question can be, "have you ever hiked MT. Kilimanjaro? I hear people say its mad fun"

"Do you like this type of music? If not, then which one do you like?

Sooner or later, the two of you will start talking about something different than this. And that is how friendship is born.

Small Talk Decoded: Never Ask These Questions

Have you ever asked a question that made you feel like a total loser? Well, here are 5 questions to never ask when trying to build up a conversation.

"Did You Come Here For Fun?"

This question tends to pop up often. Please, you had better not ask it when it does. A variation of this question is meeting someone who indicates they had a trip to such and such places. For example, "Last week I went to India", and then you ask, "Wow, cool. Did you go to have fun?" Answer: "Actually it was my father's burial". Alternatively, someone tells you, "I came here last week." You respond, "Oh, I love it here, total fun" to which they reply, "Well, I came here to get a second opinion on cancer."

Rather, ask: "What was the reason for coming here" or "What took you there?"

"Is This Your Sister/Mother/Daughter?"

You may think you know the relationship between two people you have met, but you could be wrong. You may ask a guy whether that is his daughter, and he responds, "She is my fiancée, in fact".

Instead of asking such questions, ask better questions such as,

"And who is this gorgeous lady I am honored to meet?"

"And When Are You Going To Have Kids?"

This sounds like a popular, inoffensive question; but it is. Especially when the person has been trying to conceive without success, your question then becomes a salt on their wound. Don't ask such a question unless the other person brings up such a conversation.

"For How Long Have You Been Dating?"

This question can automatically come out of your mouth when you meet your long time friend who brings a woman with him. But oops, who told you they are dating? They will just look at each other and awkwardly stumble out a vague answer. Instead ask, "How long have you known each other?", or "How did you meet?"

Bonus Tip: never start a conversation that concerns the other person's weight, or make small talk concerning someone else in that room, bus, bar, conference etc.

Now that you know how to start small talk, let us now look at how to start a conversation after the small talk and keep the conversation going.

Chapter 5.

Conversation Decoded: The Art of Conversation

In this chapter, we are going to focus on the art of starting and maintaining a conversation with a stranger. Conversation as a form of communication tends to be less formal and more spontaneous. Basically, we enter into conversations for purposes of pleasant interactions in order to meet new people, gather information, and enjoy social engagements. Types of conversations vary from intellectual conversations and exchange of ideas, to friendly debate and witty banter.

For someone prone to experience social phobia, the biggest challenge tends to be how to start a conversation and how to keep it going. Naturally, it's normal to struggle a bit while trying to make small talk since it's not easy to think of what to say. However, when it comes to anxious people, this may worsen to an extent of talking too much, which may have a negative impression on others. Therefore, let us look at how you can start a conversation with strangers easily.

Tips On How To Start A Conversation With Strangers

The hardest part in socializing, especially for those experiencing social phobia, is starting a conversation. Nonetheless, it is completely wrong to go about life content with not making first moves and only waiting for other people to do it.

Below are some tips you should follow to help you start a conversation: When starting a conversation, it's always good to say something general and not too personal. For instance, talking about the weather, "lovely day, isn't?" giving a compliment "that jacket looks good on you", making an observation, "I have just noticed you are reading a book about swimming, do you like swimming? To introduce yourself, "I don't think we have met before, I am…"

You don't have to say something witty. It's good to be genuine and sincere.

Talk about common things "how old is your son? My daughter started walking just a month ago, is your son walking yet. Talk about pets, "do you prefer a puppy or a cat? My puppy is really stubborn."

Talk about current events, "hey, did you hear about the missing helicopter? That was strange."

Bring up an old conversation, "do you remember my

college best friend, Jane? She just got married two days ago."

Ask easy to answer questions; some questions are a bit complicated, has someone ever asked you something like, "what are your weekend plans" and felt like, "do I really have to answer this?" Instead of asking that, ask something like, "what are you up to today?", "how is work today?"

After you start a conversation, you want to keep it going. In this regard

Tips On How To Keep A Conversation Going

One of the major challenges you are likely to face when socializing is the awkward silence. Awkward silences make you feel uncomfortable to a point where you feel compelled to avoid going to social places in the first place. However, here is how to get around it: Avoid Filtering: this reflex allows you to say anything that arises in your mind. No filtering, no confirming with yourself, "How will I sound if I say this?" Well, the best way to get used to this is by exercising it on people you are familiar with; it feels comfortable when you realize no one is judging you. As long as you don't say something that can jail you, then that's okay.

"Interesting, Tell Me More!" this will often work 99%. It tends to be a surefire technique for socially phobic people. Everyone loves to know that you are interested in what they say; if you show interest, they will want to talk to you more and more. Expressions like, "oh! That's interesting...", "Hmm, I have never heard of that before", "Hmm, awesome!" are reactionary parts of conversations that prove to others that you are really listening and makes them feel flattered.

People Know when you tell them stories that juice-up conversation, and when you talk about your own stories. You don't have to draw stories from your experiences when talking to others.

Choose stories mostly discussed on TV, radio, magazines, etc. The key to integrating this into conversation is by showing others that you have heard the story, and how interesting or weird you found the story.

Of course a conversation will end, so don't become too nervous or feel rejected when a conversation nears its end.

Tips For Ending A Conversation

Running out of things to talk about does not mean you have failed or you are boring. In these instances, you need to end an interaction gracefully.

Here is how to go about it…

End conversations with an excuse, For instance, you can say something like, "Sorry I have to catch up with someone at the party," or "Sorry, I have to get back to work."

Offer an apology. "I don't want to keep you longer; it was nice talking to you."

Make a suggestion. "How about we meet and talk more about this next week on Tuesday?"

Chapter 6

7 communication techniques and tactics to win small talks

1. Personal Charisma

"Words have magic and the way we articulate them, has magic too."

Conversation manners not only communicate personality traits but they also tend to reflect some other personal characteristics. Communication and conversation have a great significance in our lives, and the way of talking creates a lifetime impact on others. This impact compels others to listen and it is a key trait to one's personality as it leads to success and acknowledgement. This personality trait is called personal charisma. Charisma means magic; a spell which enforces others to ponder upon your communication and makes your conversation worth listening and appealing.

Personal charisma is the magic of one's personality and is that person's way of talking. Charisma is a constellation of complex and sophisticated social and interpersonal skills. This charisma allows influencing others at the deeper level of emotions and creates strong relations with concrete foundations. Charisma brings the following features to one's personality:

• Emotional Expression

People who have charisma in their personality, communicate and express their feelings more genuinely and impressively. This manner of their personality makes them affect others' moods and helps them be convincing on every matter. People use to trust this kind of people more compared to those who do not have a charismatic personality.

• Emotional Reliability

Personal charisma makes individuals more positive towards other people. Those individuals can respond to others' emotions in a healthier manner, and they can get more satisfaction and peace of mind. Other people rely on them for their emotional needs, and that gives them confidence and courage to do more for others and that's why we can see that good social worker are mostly good speakers.

• Self-control

Where personal charisma allows others to trust the charismatic individuals, it also gives these individuals, more control of their emotions. Personal charisma inculcates a balanced flow of emotions in charismatic personnel, making it possible to deny the importance of self-control in our day-to-day life.

• Healthier Relations

Personal charisma makes one able to have healthier relationships as compared to others who don't have a personal charisma and therefore are not able to understand others, and their points of views and also to pursue others on their own viewpoints. Having a personal charism is an extremely positive thing in a relationship since the understanding level is high then there will be a little chance of confrontation which allows for a social acquaintance to cherish.

We also need to keep in mind the type of conversation and to participate accordingly. We will discuss some of the major types of conversation in the next key, along with their main characteristics.

2. Types of Conversation

Personal charisma is important for a successful conversation, but one must not forget to consider the scenario and the type of conversation in order to act accordingly. Conversation tactics is a vast topic to describe and are also categorized in kinds. Conversation tactics have a complete structure just like every profession and situation have its own conversation tactics. We will explain some of them below:

• Casual Conversation

Casual conversation refers to a conversation undertaken in a carefree manner. This kind of conversation is commonly used among friends and family members. While talking to the ones close to us, we don't have to be so careful about the discourse, and we don't have to be so conscious although we must respect the basic codes of conduct and ethics.

• Formal Conversation

Formal conversation is used in public gatherings and feasts when you have to meet so many people and keep the element of prestige and positive attitude in your conversation. In a formal conversation, we have to be conscious about your every word.

• Professional Conversation

Almost 90% people of us are professionals in any aspect of job or business and have to spend most of our time in professional life. Professional life has its own demands, and the most essential of those demands is the use of perfect professional language and jargons that are required in a profession. According to our professional needs, we have to develop our conversation tactics. For example, a doctor, has to use specific and polite conversation tactics, but a judge, should have element of strictness and discipline so as to keep the house in order and establish an esteemed image.

• Counselling

Counselling is also a conversation tactic. This kind of

conversation is greatly admired and used by psychotherapists in an attempt to help people solve their minor problems with healthy and fruitful conversations. Counselling is the most effective type of conversation with the power to create huge impact.

• Speech or Passive Conversation

This type of conversation is mostly used in political or religious addresses. Speakers have to deliver what they want to say despite thinking that what they are saying has a spontaneous flow of emotions.

Moving towards the development of conversation tactics; the next key will concern the main tactics that help improve one's conversation ability that is expressed in the best possible manner.

3. How to Develop Conversation Tactics

Once we know the primary types of conversation and their respective requirements, we can better use conversation tactics. These tactics are the rules that anyone can learn at any stage of their life. Some of these are explained in this section.

• Listening

It is an old saying that good listeners are always good speakers. Listening is the key to developing conversation tactics. Listening is somehow a wonderful way to inculcate best tactics of conversation in a sort of conversation setting where people are sharing their views and perspectives, and you are paying attention to what they are saying. That, subconsciously makes you a good speaker because you are paying attention to your surrounding and that helps you understand and respond accordingly. Good listening makes you focus on undivided focus, question and nods of agreements and disagreements that are essential for understanding and proper communication. Ultimately, these focal points will also sharpen your speaking skills.

• Knowledge of The Audience

In order to be a good speaker and to master your conversation skills, you must know your audience who you are talking to and what kind of language you have to use in that particular conversation. With professionals, you have to be careful to:

• Include Empathy

Empathy means accepting other people's viewpoints without feeling reluctant or resistant to others; respecting and granting everyone freedom of speech. When you are empathetic during your conversation and show convincing behavior towards others, you will be more attractive to others. Empathy and equality are basic conversation tactics that give you an opportunity to be popular.

• Having Positive Attitude

Having a positive attitude in conversations makes others trust you more. When you keep a more positive and friendlier attitude towards other people and show acceptance to their ideas and thoughts, people will be less hesitant towards you. There always some incidents in life when people come to you wanting to share their worries or asking for advice. A positive attitude A positive attitude gives you the courage to be more neutral in your attitude and behavior in such cases.

• Be Assertive

Assertive means to be more honest in defining what you need and what you want in a lucid manner. Assertiveness is a key skill in your conversation tactics which makes your talk balanced and humble and people find you more genuine in your conversation which results in believing in you.

• Paying Attention to Audience's Body Language

People always show some kind of body language and gestures during a conversation, and this includes nonverbal signals and vibes. The human mind can interpret those signals and can understand most of other people's feelings during a conversation. So always try to pay attention towards what their body language shows and learn what people think during a conversation.

• Be Friendly and Humble

We notice in our daily life that people seem to be more attracted towards those who are more friendly and humble in their talking style. Friendly behavior makes you popular among you audience and makes other wanting to talk and share their views and problems with you as they feel comfortable while talking to you.

• Avoid Discrimination

This is the basic rule of conversation; non-discriminatory language should always be used during a conversation followed by a neutral body language. If you discriminate in your talking style, you will gradually lose your attraction and people will feel hesitated while talking to you.

• Be Responsive

Be responsive implies that you contribute to the conversation. Body language plays a vital role in the effectiveness of any conversation, and when you respond to your speakers, you show your presence and polishing your conversation tactics.

• Be informative

We usually notice in our daily life that some people seem very talkative and less beneficial than others. Always try to be beneficial to others and use the type of conversation that provides the other person with some kind of knowledge. In this way, people will respect you and listen to you.

• Be Logical

Without logic and reason, any kind of conversation and negotiation will end up in vain. Being logical and giving reasoning in a conversation makes your negotiation priceless and informative for others.

• Converse Smartly

Try not to use difficult vocabulary in a conversation. Be smart and impart ideas to others in a coherent manner. Be smart in your conversation to catch the maximum attention of your audience and people will respect and accept your ideas.

• Practice Emotional Intelligence

Emotional intelligence allows you to recognize and organize your emotions in conversations as most people try to focus more on appearances and expressions during a negotiation and to demean others. Emotional intelligence makes you aware of how to be more attractive without demeaning and how not to ignore others. It allows you to act wisely in situations where you have to be neutral and teaches you how to balance your emotions.

• Be Open-minded

Open mindedness is a worthy attribute of any conversation and makes you willing to walk away without any disturbance or confrontation if you have to face any opposition during negotiations. Open mindedness also makes you understand any possible opposition that can occur and helps you reach a conclusion.

• Be Patient and Calm

Patience and calmness of mind are essential in every aspect of a fruitful and peaceful conversation. Sometimes people openly oppose you or try to confront you, and if you do not keep calm the situation will worsen, and you will lose your audience. Rushing through such a situation or losing your temper may lead to worsening the situation and people losing their trust towards you. Also, if you have patience, you will be able to deal with anxiety and fear.

• Think Before You Speak

Your words determine what you are and where you stand in any situation and always ponder upon your words before articulating them otherwise you will have to pay for your words. Wise and useful words are always admired and praised by others, and if you speak without determining that either your words are consoling or hurting for the listeners, you will demolish your image.

• Don't Be Reluctant or Confused

Confusion and reluctance will minimize your chances to

win audience's hearts. Strengthen your way of talking and be confident on what are you trying to say and stick to your purpose of conversation otherwise you will not be impressive to others.

In a professional environment, global and social conversation tactics are required to achieve the best results. The next Key focusses on them.

4. Workplace, Global and Social Conversation Tactics

There are some norms of professional conversation that one must follow; some important tactics to become a better participant in a professional scenario in this modern global village. It is an old saying that humans are social beings and due to that we have a personal and a social need to communicate with each other. In all fields of our life, we have to communicate with others and not just with our family and friends but with our colleagues at work, with our fellows at travel. Thus, conversing is a basic need like food and air, without communication, we cannot survive this world. Nowadays, people are communicating all around the world without being conscious about their nationalities and set of beliefs.

Effective communication skills and worthy conversation tactics always strengthen your social circle. Effective communication skills make people love having you around and enjoy listening to you. Workplace conversation tactics are necessary; the office is not only a place where you spend time or go to earn money, but it is a grand social environment where you build relations with your coworkers, and you get to know your surroundings. It is really important for people to forge a positive image on others at their workplace. In any profession, your way of talking says a lot about you even if you are going to get a promotion or a bonus. Your progress at your workplace is 90% determined by your ethics in your conversation and the way you present yourself to others.

Researchers found that people who are better than others in their official conversations are more likely to be progressive in their profession. In this era of competition, people are more prone to get knowledge of conversation tactics. Suppose you are working in a company, and you have to deal with clients throughout the day, if you have good conversation tactics, clients will automatically be attracted to you, and this will increase the company's revenue. Good workplace tactics also allow you to convey your suggestions and share your views with your boss in an effective way and prove yourself to be a competent person.

Nowadays people at various workplaces, employees are specifically trained on how to deal with their clients. Employers try to make their employees good speakers and listeners. Many companies and business organizations are now making their social media sites and helplines where conversation tactics are essential to satisfy the customers or clients, and verbal communication is necessary to guide the customers. Most companies and individuals are now connected through social media applications like Facebook or WhatsApp which are easy and convenient to use. Professionals are making a difference in their workplaces because of their communication skills.

Thus, we can say that workplace tactics have a vital role in professional progress and growth in order to be good and effective professionals we have to learn those workplace conversation tactics.

Professional, conversation tactics are explained below in a more detailed way:

• Listening to Your Coworkers

Any type of conversation requires listening to others. Conversing and negotiating with others on professional matters requires good conversation skills. If you have good skills, you are better equipped to encourage people to adopt your viewpoints.

• Don't be Reluctant to Ask for Help

Nobody is perfect, and only time is required to gain skills relevant to any particular profession. Similarly, conversation tactics develop over time. You should always ask seniors for help and remember to keep the element of respect in your accent; this strategy develops a healthy relationship between you and your coworkers and ensures a friendly environment at your workplace.

• Be Appreciative To Your Colleagues

Appreciation plays a vital role in every profession. The strength of work can be doubled through encouragement and appreciation. Always adopt an attitude of appreciation towards your coworkers. Researchers said that some professionals, work for recognition and acknowledgement instead of money. Appreciative behavior towards your coworkers develops everlasting bonding among you and them.

• Be Responsive During Official Negotiations

Official meetings and negotiations always require more attention, and you must try to respond to your coworkers during meetings. Body language should be vigilant and attentive even in meetings. Lazy and less attentive body language plays a vital role in your career growth, as sometimes you can also feel like that you are not understanding a situation thoroughly but have to act the contrary.

• Utilize Quality Time in Conversations

Speedy conversations and talking in a quick manner can create confusion while conversing in brief and a quality conversation is always welcoming in professional environments. To be a logical speaker, you must take your time on thinking logically and briefly rather than spending time on long and haphazard conversations.

• Keep a Record of Happenings

As a professional, one must keep a record of important

facts and files to cope up with professional life challenges. This attitude will also help you in setting your short term and long term goals. A record keeping strategy always keeps you connected with others in the sense that other people will always find assistance and guidance in you if they need to retrieve information.

• Planned Conversations

Professionals try to be clear and transparent in their conversations, and a way to do it is pre-plan conversations. For example, to organize your ideas and thoughts so as for the concept to be clear.

• **Be Welcoming Towards Others' Views**

It is in human nature that our thoughts and views always vary from person to person. You should always keep welcoming behavior towards other people's views. Try to take criticism positively and keep in mind that improvement is a never-ending process. Be positive towards others' opinions and evaluate the feedback wisely so as to make room for improvements. When you talk to your coworkers, remember to be responsive and not reactive or emotional.

• Don't Be Over-reactive

Sometimes there is silence in a conversation. Be comfortable with it and do not rush to talk like this will be considered over-reaction and your image will be tarnished. So be professional and keep your emotions in control during professional conversations.

• Remember Your Coworkers' Names

Try to address your coworkers with their names as this strategy will get you closer to them and create healthy friendships at your workplace.

• Give Compliments

Throwing compliments is a way to maintain relationships. But remember, words and facial expressions should match while giving compliments.

• Ask Open-ended Questions

Avoid close-ended questions because this will minimize the opportunity to talk and lower interest during a conversation. Ponder upon your pronunciation while asking a question and give your companions a chance to talk with you in an attempt to develop their interest in a conversation.

• Pay Attention

You must pay attention to what is being said. Your body language must be positive and reflect your interest in the ongoing conversation. Body language is pivotal in verbal communication. People read others' gestures and expressions during a conversation to judge the level of interest in the subject and commitment. An apparent disinterest in the conversation is read negatively and is considered a careless attitude in official negotiations and dealings.

• Try to Make Your Conversation Interesting

Even in professional life, people want to have interesting conversations rather than boring official meetings. So being a well-versed speaker means that one is able to make their conversations interesting and draw attention during business meetings of presentations. By doing this, you will find that your coworkers and your colleagues are responding in a more attentive and healthier way.

• Time Your Conversation

Timing is crucial; you should practice timing your conversations. Let others elaborate on their thoughts. It is important that you let others convey their message completely. Neither does anyone like to be interrupted in between nor can you understand the actual meaning of what you hear. If you can understand the actual viewpoint of others, you can explain your ideas better. Timing is, therefore, a vital conversation tactic for all kinds of negotiations and dealings.

• Keep Yourself Updated

It is important that you have information about the current situation, recent events, and important developments. You should be able to respond to any references possibly made during a conversation. Many people are habitual of bringing current affairs and latest developments in fields of common interest into the conversation just to make them more interesting. You should keep yourself updated so that your conversations are more interesting and informative. A quick scan of newspaper headlines with your morning latte should prove helpful.

Apart from the news, keep your calendar updated for birthdays, homecomings and other social events and happenings in your circles. Professional relationships develop better in a friendlier environment; it is important that you maintain a certain level of openness with your coworkers.

• Be Language Learned

Linguistic literacy is a significant conversation tactic in the globalized world of the twenty-first century. The growing interconnectedness of individuals from various countries, cultural and racial backgrounds has increased the importance of multilingualism. It is difficult for a person to manage his professional dealings if he as clients who cannot converse in his native language. As a global citizen, you should be versed in more than one languages to make conversations more convenient and productive. To overcome the language barriers, the United Nations made English into a compulsory second language for all the member nations. The measure has helped in reducing linguistic barriers to a certain extent, making English the global Lingua Franca; however, the role of linguistic literacy in the establishment of stronger professional relationships remains critical. A subjective factor is the pattern of human nature which shows that people tend to be more open to those foreign nationals who can converse with them in their own language instead of a second language like English.

In the twenty-first century, globalization is a reality and the need for every country to survive in this transformed system of the socio-economic and political environment, and so linguistic literacy is an important conversation tactic. You should be literate in at least two languages to manage your professional relationships and dealings well.

• Develop Acquaintance

It is quite difficult to persuade a stranger to agree with your viewpoint. One should always develop a certain level of acquaintance with others before trying to convince them of anything. Some people might be neutral to a discussion with a stranger but may not approve his endeavours to bring them round to his point of view; however, if they understand a little of his nature through some initial conversation, it is more likely that they will participate willingly in the exchange of ideas while one tries to persuade rather than being offended by it. It is a common observation that people tend to pay more attention to those who are acquainted with them; therefore, establishing a sense of knowingness is vital in persuasive conversations.

• **Use Affirmative Language**

Be clear in your meaning and try to be affirmative in your conversations. Speak less and prefer quality speaking and firm words rather than useless long talks. Avoid contradictory statements which will increase the chance of ambiguity. Speaking in a clear way will keep your intentions clear and meaningful.

• Ensure Credibility

Credibility is something you must inculcate in your

conversations. It is the quality of being trustworthy. You must know what you are talking about, never refer to any case or scenario you are not fully aware of, while making reference always use authentic and acclaimed sources and last but not the least establish your expertise and knowledge in the subject under discussion. If people find one's expertise to be sound enough, they tend to trust them more.

Always define your need in a lucid manner before others and express your self in a credible manner.

• Create Urgency

It is in human nature that if something seems urgent people are more inclined towards it. Individuals who are versed in persuasive tactics of conversations make ideas and thoughts into scarce resources and enforce urgency for their acceptance. Just as launching a product in the market without appropriate marketing and advertising cannot win a broad customer base, simply proposing an idea or thought without reasoning it, validating and establishing a sense of urgency about its acceptance and implementation one can never persuade people to agree with him. Creating urgency is an important tactic in persuasive conversations, people who can make their opinions seem appropriate for time and trends are more persuasive than others.

• Be Specific

One thought branches out to many opinions but you must use reasoning, references and examples which are relevant to your opinion. Sharing instances and impact of a certain idea on others is one of the most common persuasive techniques, but you must make it a point that the stories you tell are not irrelevant to the context of the whole discussion. Be very specific about your ideas and thoughts and advocate them concisely. If you step off the track it is quite probable that you may not be able to bring the discussion back to its original frame. While you should always be informative in your conversations, it is very important to be specific about the ideas you want to inculcate. An advocate can certainly never win a case if he speaks of an event which doesn't circumference his evidence and the line of argument. Relevance and specification are significant in persuasion.

• Be Comprehendible

Never speak too swiftly or too slowly during a conversation in general and a persuasive conversation in particular. Speak firmly and coherently. If people cannot hear every single word that you speak and ponder upon it, it is difficult for them to understand the message that is being conveyed to them. One must be audible and comprehendible in their speech to have a good convincing power. People who speak very fast generally tend to fail in persuading people to accept their viewpoint because the listeners cannot hear them clearly or interpret their words properly. You should always be fluent and firm if you want your words to have persuading power.

Contrary to speaking too fast, if you speak too slowly

people tend to get bored, negligent and diverted. If one takes too long to present their points of views and validate them, listeners might just lose the string itself. You cannot persuade a person who stopped paying attention in the middle of the conversation and that is why you should always speak firmly and coherently, fluently yet understandably.

• Talk About the Incentives

The cost-benefit analysis is done before making a choice, whether it is about investing a sum of money or it is about accepting an idea. People tend to weigh the pros and cons and costs and benefits of the new propositions. In order to persuade people to agree with your opinion, you must give them an incentive. By incentives, in general discussions, the social and financial benefits are meant. It is human nature that people always seek a return for acceptance, whether it is an offer being accepted or simply a thought. Unless you bait the fish you cannot catch; similarly, unless you give incentives you cannot bring people round to your viewpoints.

• Body Language

Your body language, gestures, postures and facial expression play a significant role in persuading people to accept your opinions. If you seem confident and aware of what you speak about, dedicated and inclined towards the idea you compel people to pay more attention to your validations and reconsider their own opinions simply because they can read your strong belief in your thoughts. Your self-confidence can persuade people. Show interest in the conversation, if others can see that you are willingly presenting your views and would like them to learn about them they listen more attentively and give a good thought to whatever they listen to. Also, people tend to be more open to others' opinions if they feel that others are welcoming to their ideas. It is, therefore, important that you must have a positive body language in order to persuade others.

Last, the choice of words is quite vital in conversations, you must choose your words wisely. Whether it is a persuasive conversation or a general discussion, it is important that you consider your words before you speak. Offending someone during a conversation or using inappropriate words can affect your communication negatively. The next Key discusses this important conversation tactic in detail.

5. Body Language

Body language is a significant component of verbal communication, and its importance has grown over time with the rapidly growing process of globalization. Globalization has its impacts on society, and cultural practices and communication is not an exception. As interactions between people from various origins and native languages take place, body language is pivotal for meaningful exchanges. Since there exist linguistic barriers, people judge the intent and commitment by observing the body language, the responsive gestures, facial expressions, and movements. Gestures and nonverbal cues play a significant role during negotiations, and an individual with good communication skills can read gestures even if he cannot understand the language.

Body language is a core conversation tactic, and it is not only used by humans but animals as well. Body posture, eye movements, and facial expressions coherently express the emotions and sentiments of the conversant. Sign language is a form of body language which is used to convey messages by those who cannot speak; this fact highlights the significant impact that body language has on our conversations. Gestures and movements are more powerful tools of expressing thoughts and ideas as compared to speech at times. A human can naturally interpret other humans' body movements, and facial expressions and a person with sound communication skills can easily read others' thoughts on a matter simply observing their body language during a conversation. It is convenient to observe if one is interested in the conversation, uninterested or irritated by the exchange.

Interpretation of gestures and body movements varies greatly from country to country or from situation to situation, for instance; a thumbs up can be taken as a good luck wish or a signal towards the top. Interpretation of body language is subjective though.

Understanding and interpretation of body language are a vital skill in many professions such as applied psychology and criminal investigation. Communication is a key human practice and body language greatly impacts people's conversations. The study and systematic knowledge of body language are formally known as kinetics. Kinetics was first introduced by the American Anthropologist, Ray Birdwhistell. In the modern globalized world of today, the knowledge of kinetics is very important. Kinetics is a wide knowledge, and some of its most important parts are:

• Emblems

Emblems are the easily interpretable signals coming from the use of body language. They are comprehensible and can be directly translated into a sentence or a phrase. Emblems are the most easily recognizable form of gestures and body language. For example, the sign "V" with the help of hand and fingers can be easily interpreted as a victory. Same as the sign "O" is interpreted as good or okay. These are the easily interpretable signs we use to express our feelings in our daily lives.

• Illustrators

Illustrators are those signals of body language which reinforce the nonverbal signals to be translated in a verbal form and can be ambiguous and vary from place or situation. For example, pointing at someone or something the conversation is about. Illustrators are reinforcing signals. The use of illustrators is a common practice in Anglo-Saxon cultures which have no refined code of conduct, but in Asian cultures, use of illustrators is considered as a lack of intelligence.

• Regulators

Nonverbal signals which are used to regulate, moderate and keep the flow of a conversation are known as regulators in kinetics. They are often used to give feedback if the viewpoint of others has been clearly understood. For example, in some civilizations people use to nod their head and produce the sound of 'uh' 'uhhu' to show their understanding, in some other countries people use silence to express understanding. In our daily life, we use a lot of examples in conversations, and when a person wants to interrupt, that person raises their hand so as to indicate his/her need to interrupt or to say something. In response usually, a nod is used to grant permission to the other person to speak and share their thoughts. The gesture as a tool to regulate the flow of the conversation and passing on the opportunity to speak to the other side without actually making an intervention that would break the flow.

• Adaptors

Adaptor shows the postural changes and other physical movements during conversations as the posture tells much about the interest or lack of understanding. If you see a person sitting in a fatigued or uncomfortable manner that person is showing a lack of interest. If a person sits in a vigilant manner, it shows the interest and understanding of the conversation. Adaptors are easy to understand and important part of kinetics that helps to polish your conversation tactics.

• **Affect Displays**

An action or affect display is the ultimate part of kinetics as it directly shows emotions. Some researchers say that the leg movement defines true feelings. We often see some people moving their legs while talking and this shows their understanding or their level of interest. Similarly, open and relax body posture shows the confidence. Thus, we can say that posture shows the moods, status, approval, warmth and other emotions.

All these types of body language define the complete knowledge of body language. Body language is essential in conversation tactics. We always use some kind of body language during our conversations as without this attribute our conversations can be as monotonous or boring as robots.

The conversation has a major objective, which is persuasion. In the next key, we are going to have a look at the ways we can persuade the listener.

6. How to Persuade the Audience.

Body language performs one major function which is to persuade others by complimenting words. If body language does not complement words, people would not believe anything that is being said. It is important to persuade listeners. Being persuasive means to convince people to accept your viewpoints. Persuasive conversations are the most interesting kind of conversations as they involve proposition and opposition of ideas where good conversation skills tend to win. Disagreements can occur at any point during a conversation and may lead to a sudden loss of confidence. It is, thus, important to develop persuasiveness.

If you are persuasive in your conversations, you can inspire trust to others very quickly. It is a tactic used by every good speaker. Persuasiveness is by no means a trick; it is a conversation tactic. It is a compound of voice quality, postures, and gestures, vocabulary and jargons, etc. It is not about winning the discussion all the time; it refers to your reactions to a disagreement. You must keep your emotions under control and reason your statements before presenting your viewpoint to others. Also, an over-reaction to disagreements reduces the likelihood of cooperation. Your reactions must be balanced, and so, you must be persuasive in your conversations not assertive or naïve.

If you want to develop the persuasive conversation tactic, you must be very polite and rational in your behavior with others during a conversation. Always choose a strong way of talking and use examples to make others agree, logically. Try to present your views and ideas positively so that the listener does not take it as a personal offence. People are free to speak and express themselves in any way they wish and that is a fundamental human right. Whenever you start an argument in a conversation which you want to consider the fact that other people will have different opinions and if you want to persuade them in listening to yours then you should be sensitive towards their emotions and their opinions and consider their feelings. It is not easy to make others agree with you and if you want to persuade them then you must have in mind the rule below:

• **Timing is Everything**

It is not only your words and body language that persuade others but the timing of your statements as well; knowing the right time to talk and having the awareness and knowledge of how to talk so to get best results. If you want to make people agree with your point of view, you must approach them, when they are most relaxed and open to talk. I have learned through my personal experiences that people tend to be more easily persuaded when they are obliged. It is a general observation that people tend to be more welcoming to conversations and different viewpoints if they are complemented, thanked or humbled.

7. Don't Get Stuck with Words

We talked about persuasion in the previous key but remember not to get yourself in a confusing situation when you are searching for a convincing diction during a conversation. Sometimes it happens that you can get stuck with words. That could be a bit embarrassing. It is quite common to get confused when selecting words while you are trying to propose a point of view, persuade someone or simply interact with a person. Such a confusion, like getting stuck with words can interrupt the flow of a conversation, break it and create inconsistency. Inconsistent conversations are less likely to be interesting and effective. A smoother flow of words, channelling of thoughts and expression of emotions is always appreciated. Fluent and continuous conversations tend to be more compelling and meaningful since the conversers pay more attention to what is being said.

Being able to continue a discussion without confusion and getting stuck with words is a vital conversation tactic specifically during presentations, proposals and negotiations. You must be able to address the queries effectively and without breaking the flow of the conversation. In order to improve consistency and flow of your communication, you should practice the following conversation tactics:

• Preparation

Prepare for the conversation you are going to have, a presentation, a business meeting or any other important discussion. You should know your argument, have knowledge of the basic concepts upon which you are basing your proposal, have a sound reasoning to validate your opinions and ideas and have logical answers to any possible queries, cross questioning and counter argument. If you are well-prepared for a conversation you have clarity in your head and a clearer mind means a clear and more concrete elaboration. You can speak better, be more eloquent and fluent if you already know what you wish to say. Selection of words is much easier if you have an answered prepared in your mind as compared to a spontaneous response to any query or critique.

• Attentiveness

It is important to remain attentive during a conversation. It isn't queer to have a hundred thoughts popping up in your head during a discussion, ideas and reminiscences can stem from any reference, scenario or a feeling that a converser or you yourself may speak of. You must not dwell on the past or get distracted from planning something for the future while a conversation is underway. Unorganized, racing random thoughts break your concentration and make things unclear, you cannot formulate your answers under this confusion and the flow is thus disrupted as you speak in puzzle while searching for verbal fillers. Stay attentive and remain in the present so that you may listen to everything that is being said, ponder upon and respond firmly, without confusion or getting lost for words. Concentration is important for almost everything that you do and so effective conversations require concentration and staying in the present during an interaction.

• One Topic at One Time Only

Complete one topic before moving on to a new on during your discussions. If you, introduce two more topics and discuss them simultaneously, you would get confused, there would be a cobweb of thoughts and opinions in your head you would not be able to organize your thoughts to formulate an answer which would result in disruption of the conversation's flow due to difficulty in selection of words. If you completely close a topic before starting a new one you keep your thoughts in an organized stalk instead of jumbling up and consequently your brain's processing of vocabulary improves as well. Multitasking decreases human brain's power to process thoughts, the same is true for simultaneous discussion over various subject. To avoid getting stuck with words you should make it a point to concentrate your thoughts on one particular topic at one time.

• Listening

Develop a habit of listening to others. A conversation is an exchange between two people, one must learn to listen to others rather than just being listened to. Let others speak, listen to them carefully, stay attentive and contemplate on what you hear. If you listen to other people you will pick words, terminologies and jargons which you can use in your statements. It is common to know some words but not being able to retrieve them from your brain, if you listen carefully to others you might pick the words from you vocabulary which may help you convey your message more effectively and fluently.

• Concision

You should be concise in your statements, convey your message completely and coherently but do not unnecessarily long explanations. You can express your opinions and thoughts by choosing the right words, you do not need to give lengthy explanations if you have use appropriate words. Many people tend to have this habit of repeating one thing multiple times in several sentences which are literally synonymous because they think that a longer explanation is more convincing. A more appropriate instead of a lengthier explanation is needed to be more persuasive during a conversation for you can use more powerful and appropriate words in a concise statement as compared to a deliberately dragged one. If you speak concisely, you won't get stuck for words and speak more fluently and effectively.

• Honesty

Honesty is certainly the best policy. You should be honest about your opinions, thoughts, ideas and contemplations in a conversation. If you speak the truth, you speak in a natural flow and the words come smoothly. On the contrary, if you fabricate and tell made-up stories your brain must process the content you are to speak. Deliberating an answer takes time in processing, you must search for the most appropriate words in your vocabulary for you are manipulating the facts. If you speak the truth, you know what the reality is and you simply speak of it in a descriptive manner instead of a manipulative and deliberate manner which is the case if you conceal your true opinions and emotions and tell a lie. If you have nothing to say, confess it so that the conversation can move on. There is no use of keep contemplating when your instinct is not responsive. Honest responses save you from confusion and getting confused for words.

• Keep Calm

No matter how critical or difficult a conversation is, one must always keep his nerves. You must realize that the more you get worked up and anxious about a conversation the more confusing it gets. If you feel nervous or anxious about a conversation, you will always be stuck for words. Confidence is the key, you need to be clear in your head and confident about your ideas and views. If you feel intimidated by anyone, just take a deep breath before you begin. If you feel anxious about anything, your mind gets confused and its processing power decreases which results in disruption of word flow. To keep the conversation fluent, it is important to have a clear and focused mind, and for that, you must keep your nerves and stay confident during a conversation no matter how difficult it is.

• Think

You must keep the thought process flowing during a conversation to render your brain some convenience in staying vigilant about the kind of vocabulary you must use during a conversation. Staying focussed during a conversation not only channels more relevant and better thoughts relevant to the subject of discussion but helps the words flow going as well. Keeping the thoughts organized and keep thinking during an interaction are one of the most important conversation tactics for several vital reasons and a smooth word flow is one of them.

• Curiosity

Curiosity keeps you completely engaged during a conversation, develop interest in the ongoing conversation to inspire inquisitiveness and curiosity which help the thought process to stay specific to the topic. If you are curious about a topic, you will have queries and that helps you think faster and better about a subject of discussion and so curiosity and inquisitiveness help the brain channel a smoother word flow during a conversation.

• Language Proficiency

If you are proficient in a language only then should you choose it as your medium of communication for any kind of communication, personal or professional. The world is now a global village and the probability of having a conversation with an individual from a different geographical, racial and linguistic background is much greater now. In order to keep the conversation flowing without any sort of disorder and a smooth word flow it is important that conversations are done in a language of one's proficiency. It is common that people can read and write in a particular language quite efficiently but their spoken skills are weak. You must work on your spoken language skills before you use it in a conversation. Read write literacy in language differs greatly from spoken proficiency, this difference is commonly ignored by people but it matters for a smoother word flow and effective conversing. Do not use a language for official dealings and negotiations or crucial personal discussions until you have enough knowledge of the language. Linguistic literacy is very important not only for persuasiveness in a conversation but for an uninterrupted word flow as well.

• Nobody's Perfect

Always remember that nobody's perfect and it is perfectly alright to pronounce a word wrongly or make a linguistic error once in a blue moon. You should not feel inferior or be too concerned about a perfect reasoning during your conversations. Inferiority complex and overthinking about a discussion would not help you in any way, rather it will confuse you and diminish your concentration as well as thinking capacity during a conversation. It is imperative that you must think clearly and confidently for a more productive conversation and an evener word flow. You will sound better if you are confident about what you say rather than being too confused in your consciousness and anxiety of not being good or being inferior to anyone. You don't have to be perfect, you only need to convey your thoughts in the most convincing manner and for that, it is important that you do not get stuck for words.

Keeping the thought process organized, developing an interest in the conversation, being inquisitiveness and maintaining a continuous flow of ideas along with being calm, confident and honest are some of the most significant conversation tactics to maintain a smooth and uninterrupted flow of words, your choice of words is clearer if you can think clearly about a certain subject and have adequate knowledge of the language of discussion.

Conclusion

Communication is one of the most important human activities for one's survival in this world, it is a need in our daily lives. Conversation skills are required to maintain healthy relationships, personal as well as professional. Developing better communication skills is one of the most significant components of personality building and for this reason, many organizations have introduced communication skills courses in on-the-job training over the past few years. Effective communication requires certain tactics and techniques to be employed. It is important that one talks clearly and coherently with logic, reasoning, and confidence. Persuasiveness is an important skill in conversations where in order to convince people to accept their ideas and views, one must present his case in a coherent and refined manner, an uninterrupted word flow certainly improves the effectiveness and persuasiveness of a conversation. This book highlights some of the most vital conversation tactics that must be worked on so as to refine one's conversation skills and improve the effectiveness of his or her communication with others.

ABOUT THE AUTHOR

An avid admirer of the human body and a careful observer of its multiple functions, observing reactions of different people during different conversations, founder of 7 techniques and tactics to get attention of your audience or someone who you are talking to, so that you can say more by saying less words.

Mike is very experienced in self-esteem topic, currently is working on his own training course to get fit, mentally and physically, so that you can find balance in your life. In case you need any additional informations, or you would like to use any of his services, even asking questions about some tips or tricks, you can contact him on his e-mail mikebrayofficial@gmail.com and he will reply withing few hours, depend on how much work he has. Every mail is highly appreciated because you are showing that you are taking action in doing something with your life.

www.ingramcontent.com/pod-product-compliance
Lightning Source LLC
Chambersburg PA
CBHW070133210526
45170CB00013B/873